Printed in Canada

First edition October 2022

ISBN - 978-1-57571-904-7

(hardback)

Designer: Abby Williams

abbywilliamsdesign.com

SOUTHERN THESAURUS

For When You're Plumb Out of Things to Say

WRITTEN BY KELLY KAZEK

ILLUSTRATED BY JOSHUA J. HAMILTON

ABOUT THE SOUTHERN THESAURUS

In the South, language is a fluid thing. Sometimes, when we find ourselves in need of just the right word, Southerners will just make one up. And why not? It's one of our best-known talents.

All this creativity has led to a plethora of colorful and quirky words and phrases that can be used in a variety of situations.

We decided to gather these words and phrases into this handy reference book. If you're having a difficult time thinking of something to say, we've got you covered.

We can also help explain the subhead of this book: "For When You're Plumb Out of Things to Say." In our world, "plumb" has no relation to pipes or water.

It means "totally," as in "plumb wore out." You won't find the Southern meaning of "plumb" at Dictionary.com, but that doesn't mean our way is wrong.

In addition to offering alternative phrases for everything from "adorable" – cute as a bug's ear – to "underwear" – step-ins or underbritches – this book explains the origins of some of our favorite Southern words, such as "tacky," "mess" and "y'all."

Yes, we Southerners take credit for "y'all," the most useful word in the English language. Since the first colonists carelessly lost the English language's *only* second-person pronoun – thou – Americans have been fighting over what should take its place. Among those floating around are "you guys," "youse," "you'uns" and "y'all." Y'all, of course, is the most popular choice because, well, it rolls right off the tongue.

You'll also learn how to properly use the phrase "bless your heart" and how to "cuss" in Southern.

In other words, this may be the most important book you'll ever own. If not, hopefully it will make you laugh. If all else fails, it will make a great doorstop. No matter how you use it, we know you'll enjoy it!

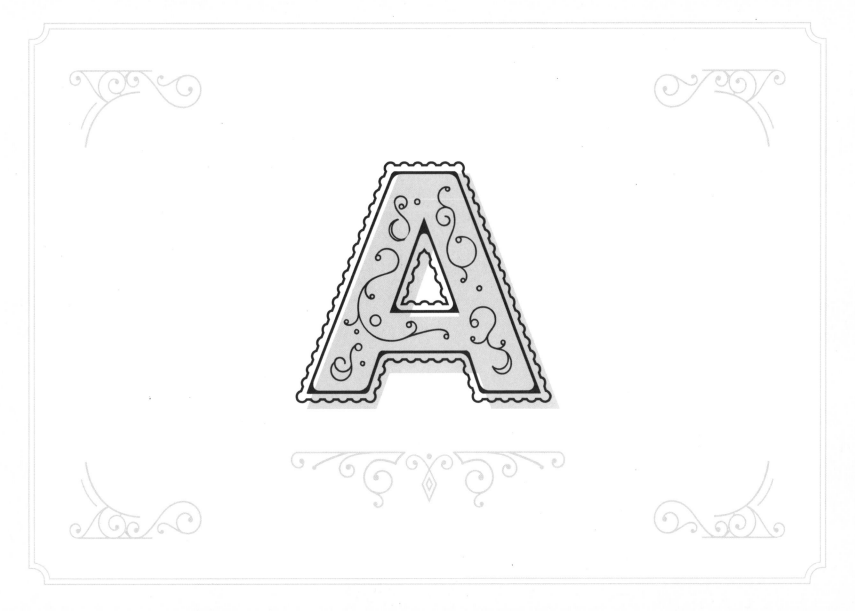

adorable

adj. *cute*

cute as a bug's ear

cute as a button

precious

could sop you up
with a biscuit

I COULD JUST SOP YOU UP WITH A BISCUIT.

NOW, USE IT IN A SENTENCE:

Suzie's granddaughter is cute as a bug's ear.   *Aren't you just precious?*   *That dress is cute as a button.*

AS ALL GET-OUT

MEANING:

To the extreme.

FOR EXAMPLE:

"She's as stubborn as all get-out!"

ORIGIN:

You've likely heard a phrase similar to this. If you're Southern as all get-out, you know it is the perfect way to add emphasis.

According to Grammarist.com: "All get-out is a mass noun which means to an extreme. It is used in comparison to another item, usually with the word as... The phrase originates in the late nineteenth century without the word *all* (e.g., as *getout*). One of the first instances of its current form in print is the 1884 American novel *Huckleberry Finn*, in which Mark Twain wrote: "all git-out."

"Get out" is not often used as a single word these days. Grammarist.com says it can be written *get out* or *get-out*.

a lot

n. *abundance*

heap

gobs

mess

oodles

Billy Bob has gobs of tools in the garage.

Aunt Sharon cooked a whole mess of collards.

Jerry is oodles of fun.

10

MORE THAN YOU COULD SHAKE A STICK AT

MEANING:

a lot

FOR EXAMPLE:

"He has more Pokémon cards than you could shake a stick at."

ORIGIN:

This phrase likely originated on farms or ranches. Years ago, sheep farmers controlled herds by waving their staffs. When too many sheep were in the herd, waving the staff (or "shaking the stick") lost its effectiveness, according to TexasMonthly.com.

alike

adj. *similar*

cut from the same cloth

go together like peas
and carrots

two peas in a pod

spittin' image

NOW, USE IT IN A SENTENCE:

Jill and Bill are cut from the same cloth.

He's the spittin' image of his daddy.

THE TWINS
ARE LIKE TWO
PEAS IN A POD.

angry

adj. *being mad*

having a come-apart

having a duck fit

get one's knickers
in a knot

fly off the handle

madder'n a wet hen

pitching a hissy fit

provoked with

riled up

DON'T GET YOUR KNICKERS IN A KNOT.

NOW, USE IT IN A SENTENCE:

Aunt Ella about had a come-apart when Jimmy Don wrecked the car.

Diddy was madder'n a wet hen when he saw the power bill.

Meemaw was so provoked with Peepaw she pitched a hissy fit.

TRANSLATING

– SOUTHERN SLANG –

Sometimes people from outside the South hear us say a word and can't quite place it – like "rurnt" or "tump." That's because we have extra special words down here, such as:

Cattywampus:

Askew, or diagonal to.

Druthers:

A person's preference in a matter.

Get up with:

To contact someone; to meet.

Gussied up:

Dressed in a fancy way.

Hankering:

A strong desire to have or do something.

High-falutin':

Pompous or pretentious.

Ornery:

Bad tempered.

Rough talk:

To speak harshly to someone.

Ruckus:

A disturbance or commotion; fight.

Rurnt:

A corruption of the word "ruined," meaning a person is spoiled or has wasted potential, as in "Her daddy just rurnt her with that new car when she turned 16."

Skedaddle:

Leave, go away quickly.

Tarnation:

Euphemism for "damnation," but typically used as an oath, in place of hell, as in "What in tarnation?"

Tickled:

To find something funny or to be pleased.

Tump:

A combination of "tip" and "dump," meaning to overturn.

Whup:

Beat, thrash.

Yonder:

Meaning "at some distance in the direction indicated," over there.

annoying
v. irritating

pestering

vexing

having one's
feathers ruffled

makes a
preacher cuss

rubs the wrong way

irksome

NOW, USE IT IN A SENTENCE:

You kids stop pestering me!

*Uncle Greg's driving is so irksome,
it could make a preacher cuss.*

16

arrogant

adj. *having an exaggerated self-opinion*

all broth and no beans

all hat and no cattle

as full of wind as a
corn-eating horse

could strut sitting down

gettin' above one's raising

high-falutin'

puttin' on airs

too big for one's britches

thinks the sun comes up
just to hear him crow

YEAH, I HEARD HIM,
BUT HE'S ALL
HAT AND NO CATTLE.

NOW, USE IT IN A SENTENCE:

*Did you hear Dwayne puttin' on airs about his new F-150?
That boy is gettin' above his raisin.'*

She always was a little too big for her britches.

Dorothy June is so proud of that hat she could strut sitting down.

TOO BIG FOR HIS BRITCHES

MEANING:

Someone is arrogant; has too high an opinion of himself.

FOR EXAMPLE:

"Kyle's been too big for his britches since he got that promotion."

ORIGIN:

May have been coined by Davy Crockett. It is found in Crockett's 1835 book, *An Account of Col. Crockett's Tour to the North and Down East:* "I liked him well once: but when a man gets too big for his breeches, I say Good bye."

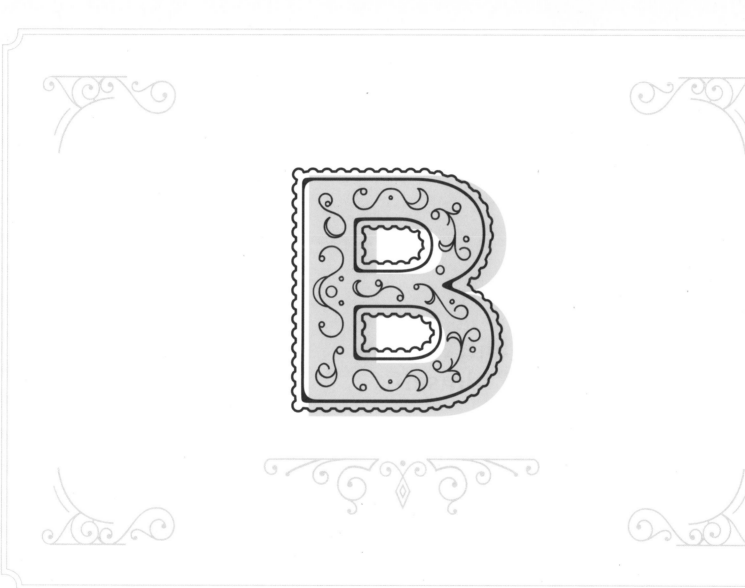

bad tempered

adj. *cross, cranky, surly*

acting ugly

cantankerous

disagreeable

ornery

JUBAL IS MORE ORNERY THAN A MULE.

NOW, USE IT IN A SENTENCE:

Emma sure was acting ugly in Sunday school.　　*Our neighbor is just cantankerous.*　　*He just likes being disagreeable.*

bar

n. *establishment serving alcohol*

dive

honky tonk

juke joint

roadhouse

watering hole

NOW, USE IT IN A SENTENCE:

Verna goes to that dive every Saturday night.

June goes to that honky tonk to listen to music.

That's Uncle Gig's favorite watering hole.

THE MUSIC IS SO LOUD, THE JUKE JOINT SHAKES.

baubles

n. *trinkets*

doodads

frippery

gewgaws

thingamajigs

trifles

whatnots

GRANDMA NEEDS MORE WHATNOTS LIKE SHE NEEDS A HOLE IN THE HEAD.

NOW, USE IT IN A SENTENCE:

You should get rid of some of that frippery at a garage sale.

You don't need any more gewgaws on your mantle.

Your mama has whatnots all over her house.

be quiet

n. *silent,* v. *attempt to make silent*

button up

hush

hush one's mouth

not a peep

shush

stow it

tick a lock

NOW, USE IT IN A SENTENCE:

Sandy told her annoying little brother to stow it.

You kids better shush back there.

His hollerin' is driving me nuts! He needs to tick a lock!

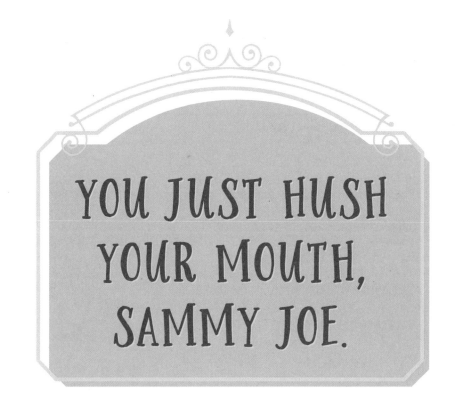

YOU JUST HUSH YOUR MOUTH, SAMMY JOE.

behave

v. comport oneself

act like somebody

act like you've got
some sense

don't show one's butt

mind one's manners

mind one's Ps and Qs

remember one's raising

JIMMY
BETTER REMEMBER
HIS RAISING.

NOW, USE IT IN A SENTENCE:

Now you go out there and act like you've got some sense.

I hope Anna Lee doesn't show her butt in church today.

Mind your manners while you're at Grandma's house.

busy

adj. *engaged, at work*

more swamped than the Everglades

running all over hell's half-acre

up to one's hind-end in alligators

NOW, USE IT IN A SENTENCE:

I've been running all over hell's half-acre getting ready for this party.

I'm so swamped at work I can't get ahead.

25

BUSY AS A FUNERAL HOME FAN IN JULY

MEANING:

Extremely busy

FOR EXAMPLE:

"Her store is busy as a funeral home fan in July."

ORIGIN:

The date of the origin of this phrase is murky, but it likely predates air-conditioning when paper fans were in common usage. It refers to the fact that people wave their paper fans continually when it's hot, and funeral homes commonly gave out paper fans as promotional materials.

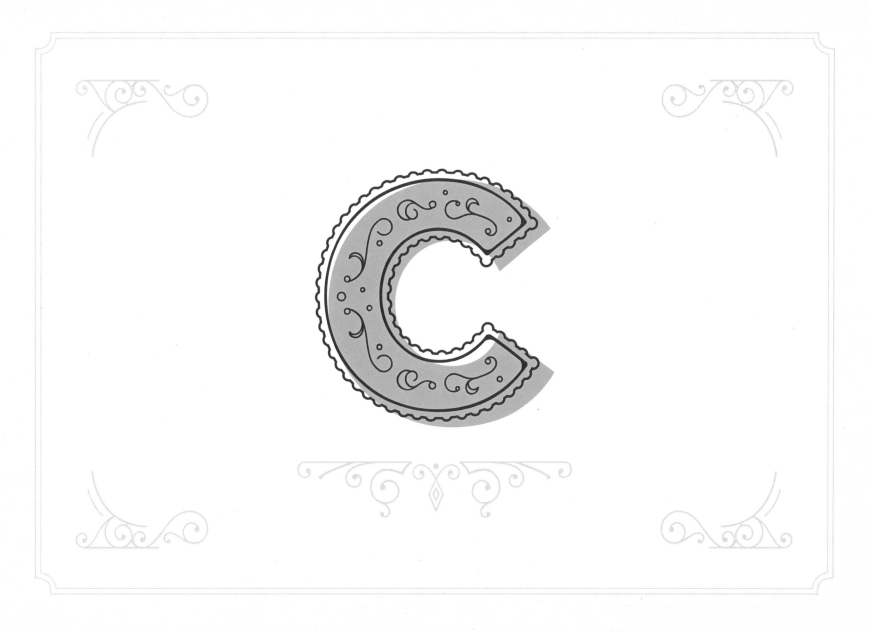

cheap

adj. *inexpensive*

skinflint

squeezes a quarter
so tight you can hear
the eagle scream

squeeze a nickel 'til
the buffalo screams

so tight you can hear
him squeak

tight as a fiddle string

tight as a wet boot

SHE KEEPS HER BUDGET TIGHT AS A FIDDLE STRING.

NOW, USE IT IN A SENTENCE:

Papaw squeezes a quarter so tight you can hear the eagle scream.

Aunt Fern is so tight you can hear her squeak.

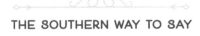

children

n. *very young people*

brood

knee-high to a
grasshopper

tadpoles

whippersnappers

young'uns

YOUNG'UNS TODAY ARE ALWAYS ON THEIR PHONES.

NOW, USE IT IN A SENTENCE:

I haven't seen Ida Jean since she was knee-high to a grasshopper.

You better keep those whippersnappers off my lawn!

The playground was just crawlin' with tadpoles.

cocktail

n. *alcoholic beverage*

hooch

libation

likker

moonshine

mountain dew

poison

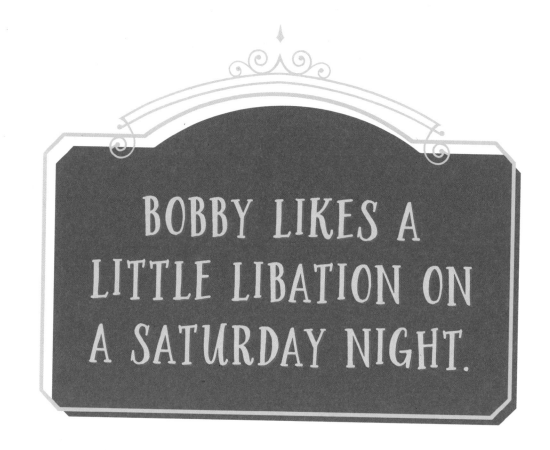

BOBBY LIKES A LITTLE LIBATION ON A SATURDAY NIGHT.

NOW, USE IT IN A SENTENCE:

It's been a long day. Got any hooch?

What kind of likker do y'all have behind the bar?

What's your poison?

cold

n. *absence of heat*

airish

as a cast-iron
commode

as a frosted frog

as an ex-wife's heart

colder than a
well-digger's butt

I'M FEELIN' AIRISH.

NOW, USE IT IN A SENTENCE:

It's cold as a cast-iron commode out here.

*When I went to Maine in December, it was
colder than a well-digger's butt.*

31

confused

adj. *mentally disoriented*

at sixes and sevens

bumfuzzled

clear as mud

discombobulated

doesn't know whether
to wind his butt
or scratch his watch

flummoxed

THAT EXPLANATION IS ABOUT AS CLEAR AS MUD.

NOW, USE IT IN A SENTENCE:

*The ending of that movie has
me completely bumfuzzled.*

*That plan really has
me flummoxed.*

*Johnny Dean doesn't know whether to
wind his butt or scratch his watch.*

crazy

adj. *acting in a wild or aggressive way*

as a betsy bug

crazier than an outhouse fly

gone 'round the bend

nuttier than a fruitcake

tetched

the cheese slid off one's cracker

y'all ain't right

THE WAY GRACIE MAY WAS DANCIN', I THOUGHT THE CHEESE DONE SLID OFF HER CRACKER.

NOW, USE IT IN A SENTENCE:

Fred was crazy as a betsy bug.

Grandma's gone 'round the bend.

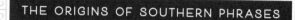

CAN'T BEAT THAT WITH A STICK

MEANING:

Can't do/get better than that.

FOR EXAMPLE:

"Two scoops of ice cream instead of one! You can't beat that with a stick."

ORIGIN:

This phrase, meaning something that can't be improved upon, stems from the phrase "you can't beat that," meaning "can't do better than that," TexasMonthly.com says. Over time, "with a stick," as if the "beating" were literal, was added for emphasis.

crooked

adj. *bent, angled*

cattywampus   whopper-jawed

cock-eyed   whop-sided

wonky   sigogglin

NOW, USE IT IN A SENTENCE:

Her hat was so cattywampus it looked like it might fall off.

The church shed was sigogglin.

THAT PICTURE IS HANGING ALL WHOPPER-JAWED.

IF TEXTING ABBREVIATIONS WERE SOUTHERN

We came up with some abbreviations we think people should be using.
Here they are with comparable phrases:

lol *(laughing out loud)* = glamec *(grinning like a mule eating corn)*

omg *(oh my gosh)* = wis *(well I swan/swanny)*

smh *(shaking my head)* = wwymt *(what would your mama think)*

rotfl *(rolling on the floor laughing)* = tarks *(that's a real knee-slapper)*

tia *(thanks in advance)* = isai *(I surely appreciate it)*

eod *(end of discussion)* = dmmcas *(don't make me cut a switch)*

imo *(in my opinion)* = mas *(mama always said)*

dgmw *(don't get me wrong)* = byh *(bless your heart)*

ttyl *(talk to you later)* = by *(bye, y'all)*

noyb *(none of your business)* = cktc *(curiosity killed the cat)*

The following abbreviations have no current counterparts, but we think they would be useful:

tjdmp *(that just dills my pickle)*   wwbdd *(what would Blanche Devereaux do?)*   hadf *(having a duck fit)*

damn

expletive

consarn it

dadburnit

dadgummit

dagnabbit

doggone it

I declare

I'll be dogged

CONSARN IT! I STUBBED MY TOE!

NOW, USE IT IN A SENTENCE:

Dagnabbit! He's late again.

I'll be dogged if Erma didn't wear white after Labor Day.

Dadgummit! You better not have scratched my bumper.

deduce

v. figure out, understand

now you're cooking with oil

now you're digging where there's taters

take to mean

NOW YOU'RE DIGGING WHERE THERE'S TATERS.

NOW, USE IT IN A SENTENCE:

You got the engine working. Now you're cooking with oil!

Do I take you to mean you plan on using Caro syrup in the pecan pie?

depart

v. leave, retreat

get on up outta here

hightail it

scat

scoot

shoo

skedaddle

NOW, USE IT IN A SENTENCE:

It's the principal. Y'all skedaddle!

Y'all need to scoot.

different

adj. *dissimilar, unlike*

a far cry from

a little off

at odds with

not quite right

off plumb

peculiar

That idea is way off plumb.

Their answer was at odds with the teacher's.

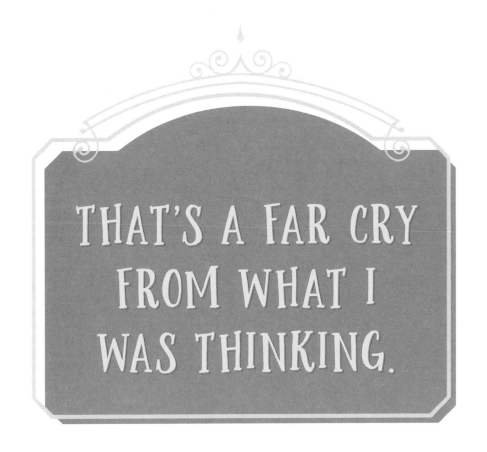

THAT'S A FAR CRY FROM WHAT I WAS THINKING.

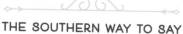

discuss

v. *talk over with another*

chew

hash over

jaw

*They were hashing
over the details of the trip.*

We've chewed on the idea long enough.

ARE Y'ALL
GOING TO JAW
ALL DAY?

drunk

adj. *intoxicated by alcohol*

as a skunk

as Cooter Brown

gassed

got a snootful

soused

tiddly

tight

HE CAME HOME FROM THE BAR DRUNK AS A SKUNK!

NOW, USE IT IN A SENTENCE:

Those boys got drunker than Cooter Brown and tore up the football field.

Otis had a snootful and was walking cattywampus.

The ladies didn't know the punch was spiked and got a little tiddly.

43

— AILMENTS —

If you've ever been "feelin' poorly," you know it's time for one of Mama's cure-all potions or salves – or sometimes just a kiss on the boo-boo will do the trick. Here are some ways we describe our ailments:

I've got a hitch in my giddyup/getalong.

He's just eat up with poison ivy.

I'd have to feel better to die.

She's wore slap out.

Grandma's feeling poorly.

She's down with the bursitis.

Grandpa's stove up (suffering discomfort from injury, illness, exercise or overwork).

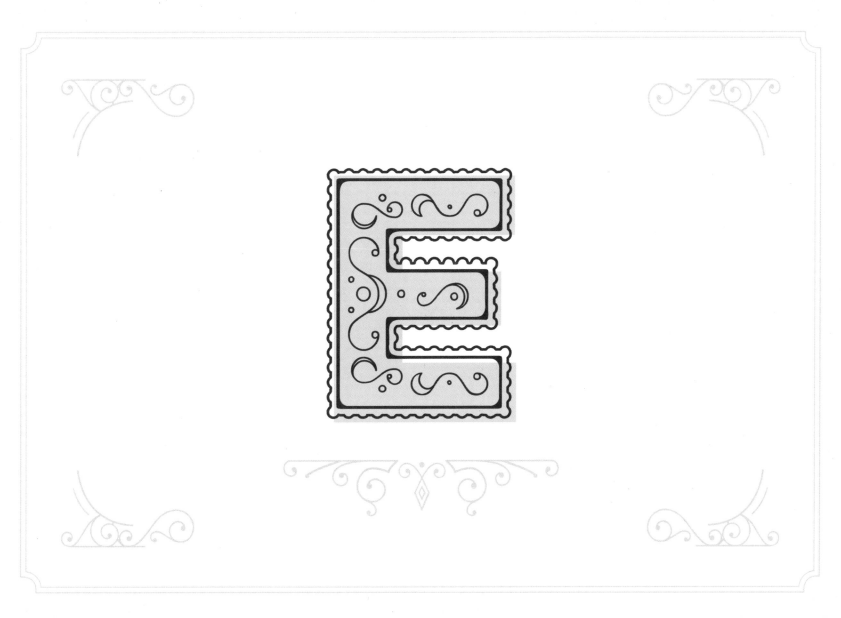

exhausted

adj. *extremely tired*

dog tired

done in

plumb wore out

pooped

slap give out

tuckered out

I AM SLAP GIVE OUT AFTER THAT PARTY!

NOW, USE IT IN A SENTENCE:

Nana was plumb wore out from shopping.

She was too pooped to even think of decorating the Christmas tree.

Ed was tuckered out after harvesting the corn.

fashionable

adj. *dressed up, dressed formally*

dolled up

done up

gussied up

in one's best bib
and tucker

THE GIRLS GOT ALL DOLLED UP FOR THE DANCE.

NOW, USE IT IN A SENTENCE:

Trudy was gussied up for the date.   *Dwight had on his best bib and tucker for the wedding.*

– APPEARANCE –

We don't insult people. That would be downright rude. But from time to time, we can't help but overhear when someone else does.

He fell out of the ugly tree and hit every branch on the way down.

He looks like ten miles of bad road.

If he were an inch taller, he'd be round.

Vern's so ugly he'd scare a buzzard off a gut pile.

She's spread out like a cold supper.

June is so ugly she'd make a freight train take a dirt road.

fight

n. *physical encounter, assault*

dust-up

rough-house

ruckus

scrap

set-to

tussle

whup

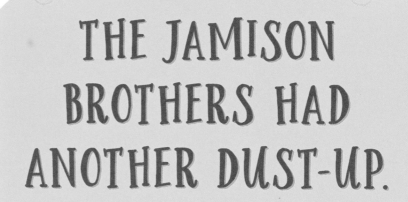

THE JAMISON BROTHERS HAD ANOTHER DUST-UP.

NOW, USE IT IN A SENTENCE:

There was quite the set-to over the referee's call.

The students caused a ruckus when the teacher left class.

They were sent to the principal's office for tussling.

food

n. *edible material*

grub

sustenance

vittles

NOW, USE IT IN A SENTENCE:

We're going to need some sustenance before going back to work.

The vittles are ready to eat.

I'LL RUSTLE UP SOME GRUB FOR LUNCH.

FAIR TO MIDDLING

MEANING:

Doing OK, average, so-so.

FOR EXAMPLE:

"I'm doing OK, fair to middlin', I'd say."

ORIGIN:

This began in the mid-1800s based on grades used by farmers to describe the quality of produce, including "good," "fair," "middling," "ordinary" and "poor," according to Merriam-Webster dictionary.

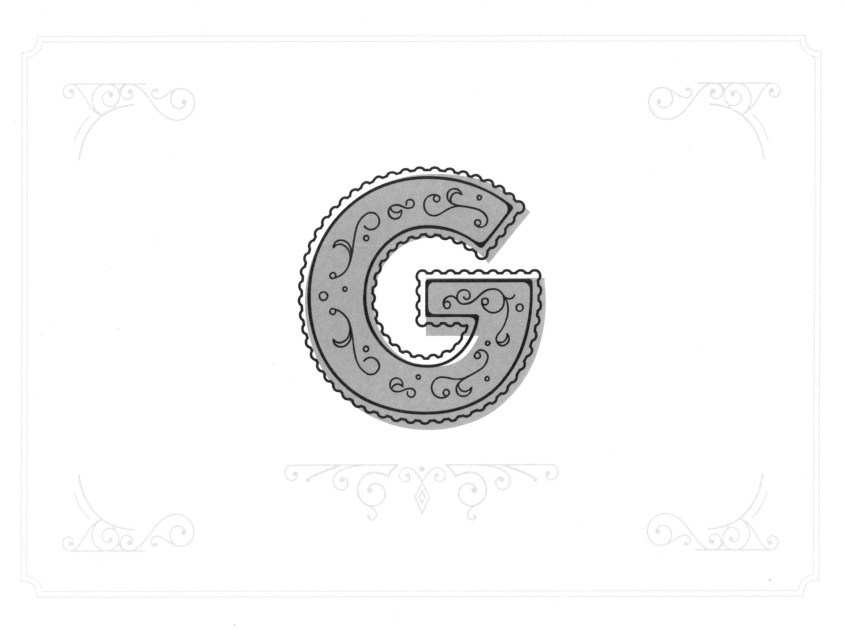

gathering

n. assemblage

hootenanny

shindig

to-do

NOW, USE IT IN A SENTENCE:

It's going to be a real shindig.

Mama wants the house clean before her to-do.

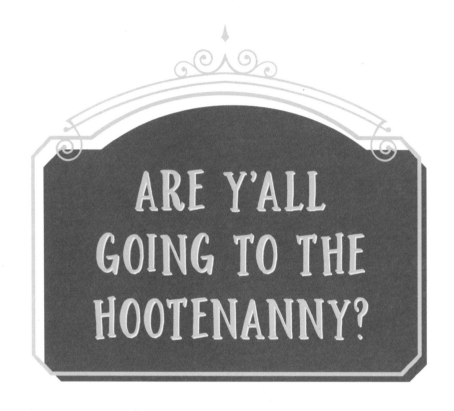

ARE Y'ALL GOING TO THE HOOTENANNY?

ghost

n. *spirit of the dead*

booger

boohag

bugaboo

haint

hot steam

night hag

plat-eye

wraith

HENRY THOUGHT THERE MIGHT BE A BUGABOO UNDER HIS BED.

NOW, USE IT IN A SENTENCE:

Sally was afraid a booger was hiding in the woods.

The spooky old house was infested with haints.

She could have sworn she saw a hot steam in the corner.

A HANDY
APPALACHIAN GLOSSARY

The Southern region of the Appalachian Mountains covers parts of Alabama, Georgia, Tennessee, South Carolina, North Carolina, Virginia, West Virginia and Kentucky. (The chain continues into Ohio and onward, all the way to Maine.)

The unique sayings, culture and charm of mountain people have been captured in numerous TV shows and films, perhaps none as well known as "The Andy Griffith Show," in which the mountain people of North Carolina play prominent roles.

We gathered some slang words used primarily in mountain regions.

Airish

MEANING: chilly

EXAMPLE: *"Get a sweater. It's airish out tonight."*

Chunk

MEANING: to throw

EXAMPLE: *"Chunk your bag in the trunk."*

Gaum

MEANING: a mess; to gaum up is to mess up

EXAMPLE: *"The floor was all gaumed up."*

Kyarn

MEANING: carrion; roadkill or rotting flesh

EXAMPLE: *"That vulture must be looking for some kyarn."*

Kindly

MEANING: kind of

EXAMPLE: *"He kindly likes the Foster girl."*

Lay out

MEANING: to be absent

EXAMPLE: *"He laid out of work today."*

Mushmelon

MEANING: cantaloupe

EXAMPLE: *"I hope this mushmelon is not too ripe."*

Palings

MEANING: fenceposts

EXAMPLE: *"Pa wants you to repair the palings."*

Reach me

MEANING: hand me

EXAMPLE: *"Reach me the screwdriver."*

Sigogglin

MEANING: not built correctly; crooked, lopsided

EXAMPLE: *"That old house is sigogglin."*

Skift

MEANING: something light; a light dusting of snow

EXAMPLE: *"There was just a skift of snow on the ground."*

Story

MEANING: a lie

EXAMPLE: *"Don't you tell me a story."*

Tow sack

MEANING: burlap sack

EXAMPLE: *"Just gather the nuts in a tow sack."*

Varmint

MEANING: wild animal

EXAMPLE: *"Those varmints keep eating the flowers."*

gossip

v. talk about others,
spread rumors

air dirty laundry

cut somebody up

getting the dirt on

scuttlebutt

spilling the beans

DON'T GO AROUND AIRING THE FAMILY'S DIRTY LAUNDRY.

NOW, USE IT IN A SENTENCE:

You ought not listen
to scuttlebutt.

I heard those ladies cuttin'
somebody up pretty good.

Betty Sue spilled the beans about
Mable's husband's sister's affair.

SOUTHERN ALTERNATIVES TO

— CUSS WORDS —

We Southerners mind our manners, especially when Reverend Dwight or Nana are within earshot. Here are some ways we can express ourselves while keeping it clean:

Son of a
motherless goat!

What in Sam Hill?

Dagnabbit!

I'll be dogged!

Mother of pearl!

H-E-double toothpicks

Heavens to Betsy!

Dadgummit!

Son of a biscuit eater!

Well tarnation!

I swan!

I declare!

Good gravy!

grandmother

n. *a female ancestor; matriarch*

Big Mama

Grammy

Granny

Mawmaw

Meemaw

Mimi

Nana

MEEMAW GIVES THE BEST HUGS.

NOW, USE IT IN A SENTENCE:

We've always called her Granny, but she prefers Mimi.

Nana always buys us candy.

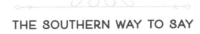
grandfather

n. *a male ancestor; patriarch*

Big Daddy

Granddaddy

Grandpappy

Pappy

Pawpaw

Peepaw

Pop

Pop-pop

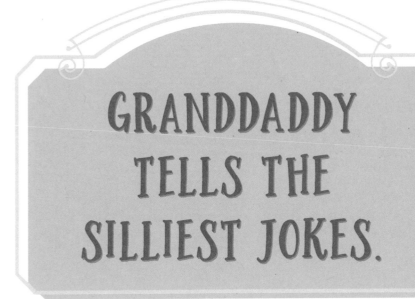

GRANDDADDY TELLS THE SILLIEST JOKES.

NOW, USE IT IN A SENTENCE:

Big Daddy wants to take us fishing on Saturday.

The kids are staying at Peepaw's house during spring break.

HIGH ON THE HOG

MEANING:

To live in great comfort or splendor; to live it up.

FOR EXAMPLE:

"After winning the lottery, Aunt Lilibeth and Uncle Pete are living high on the hog."

ORIGIN:

Stems from the fact that the upper parts of a hog are considered to provide the highest quality and most expensive meats, as opposed to parts like feet and hocks.

happy

adj. *in high spirits, satisfied*

as a dead pig
in the sunshine

as if he had
good sense

grinnin' like a possum
eatin' a sweet tater

could drop one's harp
plumb through the cloud

SHE WAS SO HAPPY SHE COULD DROP HER HARP PLUMB THROUGH THE CLOUD.

NOW, USE IT IN A SENTENCE:

Passing the test made him as happy as a dead pig in the sunshine.

News of the promotion had her grinnin' like a possum eatin' a sweet tater.

The new truck made him as happy as if he had good sense.

hijinks

n. horseplay

buffoonery

tomfoolery

rough-housing

shenanigans

NOW, USE IT IN A SENTENCE:

The principal told the students there'd be no rough-housing.

What kinds of shenanigans are they getting into today?

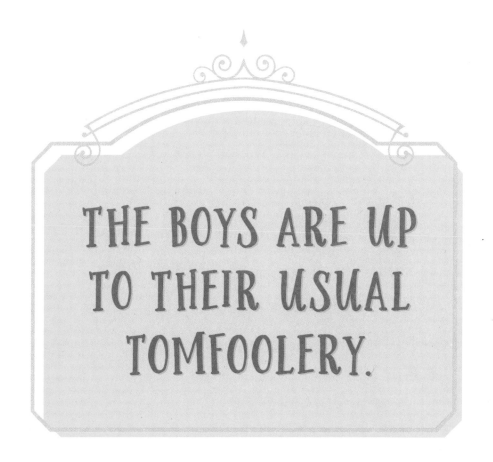

THE BOYS ARE UP TO THEIR USUAL TOMFOOLERY.

hot

adj. *having a high temperature*

as a summer revival

as the hinges of hell

hotter than a burning stump

hotter than blue blazes

hotter than Satan's armpit

so hot the hens are laying
hard-boiled eggs

IT'S HOTTER THAN SATAN'S ARMPIT TODAY!

NOW, USE IT IN A SENTENCE:

It was hotter than the hinges of hell at the picnic.

It was so hot the hens were laying hard-boiled eggs.

humid

adj. very damp weather

clammy

it's not the heat, it's
the humidity

like being hit in the face
with a wet sponge

like taking a steam bath

sultry

THE DAY WAS MORE SULTRY THAN MARILYN MONROE.

NOW, USE IT IN A SENTENCE:

It may be hot in Arizona, but it's dry heat. In the South, it's not the heat, it's the humidity.

Walking outside that August was like being hit in the face with a wet sponge.

67

SOUTHERN PHRASES TO DESCRIBE

— THE WEATHER —

Weather in the South is a hot topic of conversation – pun intended. Approach any group of people sitting on a porch fanning themselves and you'll hear some colorful descriptions of how crazy the weather is down here. Some examples:

It's hotter'n Satan's house cat.

Hot as all get-out.

That's a real frog strangler *(heavy rain)*.

It's comin' up a storm/comin' up a cloud.

It's hotter'n the devil's armpits.

So cold I saw a politician with his hands in his own pockets.

So humid it's like getting punched in the face with a sauna.

It's not the heat, it's the humidity.

It come up a gully washer *(heavy rain)*.

It come up a bad cloud *(storm)*.

It's so dry the trees are bribing the dogs.

It's colder than a well digger's butt in January.

It rained like a cow peein' on a flat rock.

It's hotter than blue blazes.

hungry

adj. *strong desire or need for food; starving*

could eat the north end of a south-bound goat

have a hankering

peckish

I COULD EAT THE NORTH END OF A SOUTH-BOUND GOAT.

NOW, USE IT IN A SENTENCE:

Ben has a hankering for some cornbread.

When is supper? Granny's feeling peckish.

HANKERING

MEANING:

Have a desire for.

FOR EXAMPLE:

"I'm hankering for MeeMaw's red velvet cake."

— or —

"I've got a hankering for some hush puppies."

ORIGIN:

The verb "to hanker" originated circa-1600, when it meant "linger in expectation." By the 1640s, it meant "to have a longing or craving for." The word may have originated from the Flemish word "hankeren" or the Dutch word "hunkeren," according to a Reader's Digest list of Southern phrases.

Word historians at Vocabulary.com and Etymologeek.com have guessed it could be related to the Middle Dutch word "hangen," meaning "to hang," which could stem from relating "hanging" or "lingering about" with longing or craving.

ill

adj. *not feeling well*

a hitch in one's giddyup/getalong

afflicted

sick as a dawg

at death's door

eat up with (disease)

feeling poorly

feeling puny

have to feel better to die

indisposed

laid up

peak-ed

too weak to whip a gnat

LAVERN WAS SICK AS A DAWG.

NOW, USE IT IN A SENTENCE:

The doctor said he had a hitch in his getalong and prescribed some pills.

Papaw was feeling so puny he said he'd have to feel better to die.

Nana was feeling peak-ed so she skipped church.

indulge

v. pamper

coddle

mollycoddle

spoil rotten

rurn

SHE'S A GROWN WOMAN AND TOO OLD TO BE MOLLYCODDLED.

NOW, USE IT IN A SENTENCE:

Their mama is going to rurn those kids.

Big Mama spoils her grandkids rotten – all 22 of them.

insect

adj. *bug*

gnat

June bug

lightning bug

love bug

skeeter

A cloud of gnats circled her head.

She was covered in skeeter bites.

JOHNNY AND SUELLEN WERE CATCHING LIGHTNING BUGS IN A MASON JAR.

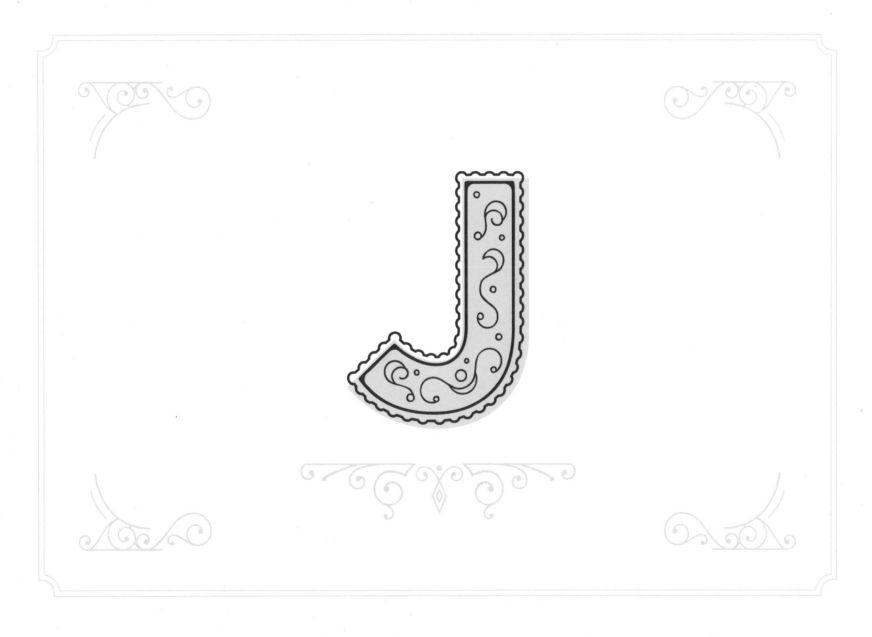

jerk

n. *mean or stupid person*

louse

lunkhead

nitwit

numbskull

son of a
biscuit eater

son of a
motherless goat

WELL LISTEN HERE, YOU SON OF A MOTHERLESS GOAT!

NOW, USE IT IN A SENTENCE:

That lunkhead put the cast-iron skillet in the dishwasher.   *Jimmy Bob is a numbskull.*   *Joan's boss was a nitwit.*

JUST FELL OFF THE TURNIP TRUCK

MEANING:

Naïve or gullible.

FOR EXAMPLE:

"You expect me to believe that? I didn't just fall off the turnip truck."

ORIGIN:

This phrase has been popular since the 20th century in the U.S., but it could have originated much earlier. It likely stems from the 16th-century belief that turnips were food eaten only by the poor or uneducated, according to NationalGeographic.com.

THESE SOUTHERN PHRASES HELP SOFTEN INSULTS

Being a polite people, we Southerners have found ways to soften insults so they don't sound like ... well, insults.

Bless your heart

EXAMPLES:

"His parents are wasting their money on tuition to that community college, bless his heart," or "Bless her heart, she's wearing white after Labor Day."

Memorable/interesting/ creative/different

This is a phrase we use when no other words get the job done.

EXAMPLE:

"The fringe on that Christmas sweater sure is memorable."

How nice for you

Everyone knows this response means: "It's nice for you. The rest of us? Not so much."

EXAMPLE:

"You have one of Elvis' toenail clippings preserved in a glass jar? How nice for you."

Can be used interchangeably with "Well, alrighty then."

God love 'im

EXAMPLE:

"The little tyke's got Spaghetti-O's all over his face, God love 'im."

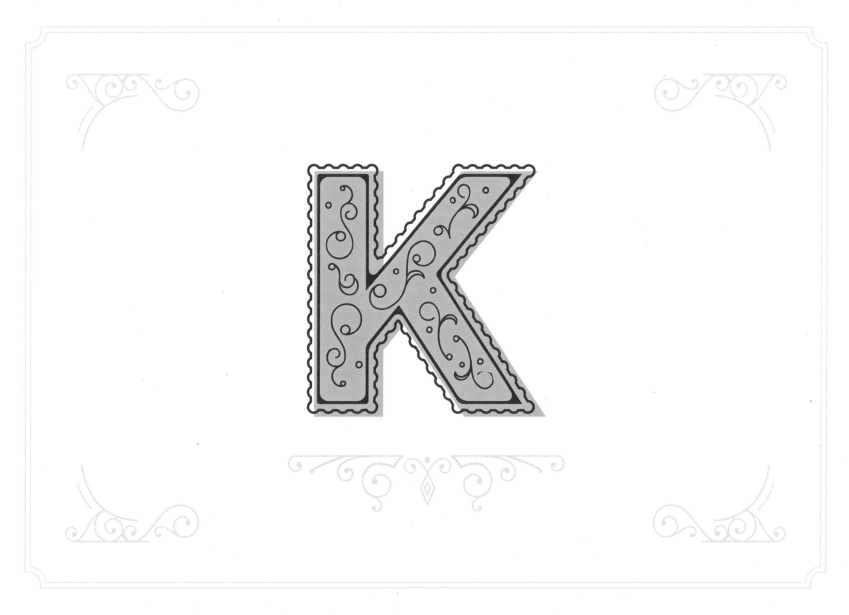

kiss

n. *touching lips to another's*

canoodle

give some sugar

smooch

NOW, USE IT IN A SENTENCE:

Those young'uns ought not smooch in public.

Give Mimi some sugar!

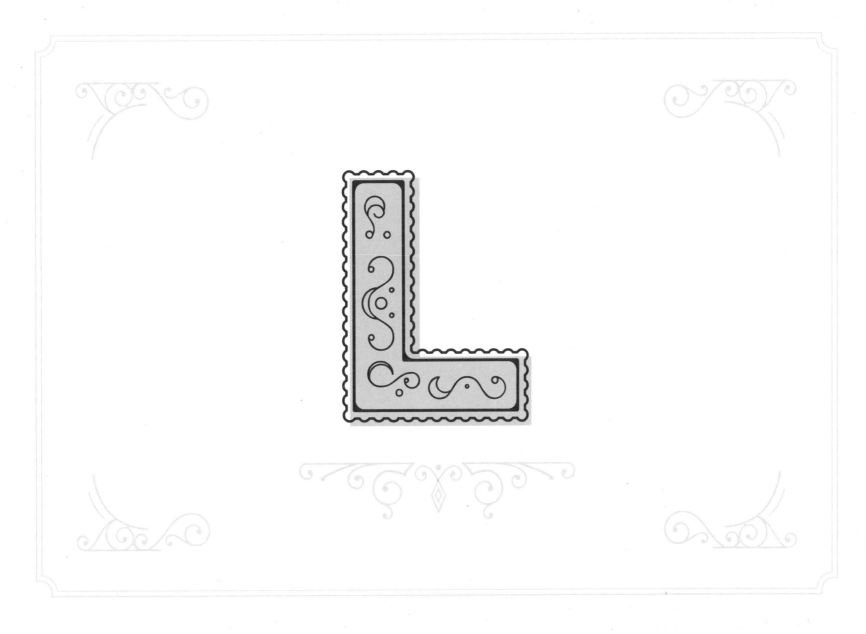

lazy

adj. *inactive, sluggish*

good for nothing

lackadaisical

no account

shiftless

slug-a-bug/
slug-a-bed

won't hit a lick
at a snake

AUNT FERN
IS SO LAZY SHE
WON'T HIT A
LICK AT A SNAKE.

NOW, USE IT IN A SENTENCE:

Tripp is a good-for-nothing husband.   *His brother is just no account.*   *I can't wake up that slug-a-bed to get him to go to school.*

lover

n. *partner or mate*

beau

honey

suitor

sweetie

NOW, USE IT IN A SENTENCE:

Queenie was single, but now she has a suitor.

I'm going on a date with my sweetie.

WHEN ARE YOU AND YOUR BEAU GETTING ENGAGED?

SILLY SOUTHERN

— ENDEARMENTS —

Do you really think plain old' "dear" is an acceptable endearment to use in the South? It isn't. Sure, it's perfectly functional, even practical. It could be used in cases when someone hasn't had coffee and is experiencing brain fog, as in "Oh, you're leaving to start college? Have fun, dear."

But for nicknames to be true Southern endearments, they need a little pizazz. A little whimsy. Some downright silliness.

Let's look at a few:

Apple Dumplin'

Or any kind of dumplin' for that matter. Apple just sounds better as an endearment than "Chicken and Dumplings."

Buttercup

In honor of the lovely daffodils that bloom in early spring.

Cat's Head Biscuit

OK, so we've never heard anyone call another person this name, but we were hoping it might catch on …

Georgia Peach

If you're from Georgia, you may have been called "My little Georgia Peach."

Goo-Goo Cluster

This one is difficult to rhyme if you're writing love poems, but it has a certain flair.

Honey Bun

This is our take on a classic ... because "honey" wasn't bold enough.

Honey Bunch

Some people stretch this out to "Honey Bunches of Oats." To each his own.

Love Bug

You may think love bugs are annoying, but it's sweet when you call someone "Love Bug."

Peach Pie

It's better than calling someone "Peach Cobbler," is all we're sayin'.

Punkin' Pie

This one is cute for kids or adults.

Sweet Pea

This one is sweet and works for kids and partners.

Sugar Lump

If you grew up with your dad calling you this, you may not think much about it. Then you get older and think, "Huh. That's a weird thing to call someone."

Shug

Short for "Sugar," this one is heard in many Southern homes.

Sugar

Use this one when referring to anyone who's sweet. Or someone you just met ... whichever.

Sweet Tater

Yes, we've really heard this. Whether the people were serious or not, we can't be sure.

Sugar Britches

Use this when you're feeling romantic.

MADDER'N A WET HEN

MEANING:

Pretty darn mad.

FOR EXAMPLE:

"Sue changed Grandma's biscuit recipe, and Mama was madder'n a wet hen."

ORIGIN:

Refers to hens dunked in cold water by their farmers to break them from a phase of "broodiness," which makes it difficult to collect eggs. The dunking, of course, tended to anger the hens.

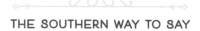

makeup

n. *cosmetics*

color

paint

put one's
face on

NOW, USE IT IN A SENTENCE:

*Mama always tells me to
put some color on.*

That woman was painted up.

JANETTE WENT TO PUT HER FACE ON BEFORE DINNER.

maybe

adv. *by chance, possibly*

as like as not

God willing

Lord willing

might could

NOW, USE IT IN A SENTENCE:

We're going on vacation this year, as like as not.

She'll graduate on time, God willing.

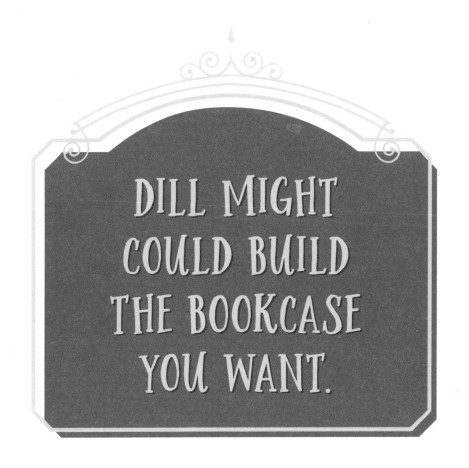

DILL MIGHT COULD BUILD THE BOOKCASE YOU WANT.

meal

n. *regular occasion for eating food*

church supper
dinner on the ground
meat-and-three
mess of somethin'
potluck
putting on the feedbag
supper

THAT RESTAURANT SERVES MEAT-AND-THREES.

NOW, USE IT IN A SENTENCE:

Each May, we have a family reunion with a dinner on the ground.

The church hosts a weekly potluck.

Nell says if we stay, she'll cook up a mess of somethin' to eat.

mirthful

adj. *merry*

jocular

tickled

NOW, USE IT IN A SENTENCE:

She was just tickled with the gift.

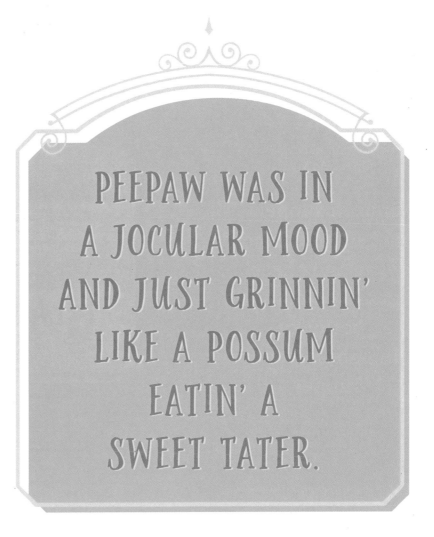

PEEPAW WAS IN
A JOCULAR MOOD
AND JUST GRINNIN'
LIKE A POSSUM
EATIN' A
SWEET TATER.

MEANER THAN A JUNKYARD DOG

MEANING:

Pretty dadgum mean.

FOR EXAMPLE:

"Don't mess with Phil. He's meaner than a junkyard dog."

ORIGIN:

This phrase didn't appear until the 20th century. It became really popular in the 1980s, and you can probably guess why: Jim Croce's 1973 hit "Bad, Bad Leroy Brown" includes the lyrics: "Badder than old King Kong/And meaner than a junkyard dog."

This one is easy to figure out – junkyard dogs are often aggressive mainly because they are usually trained to keep people from trying to steal items from the open yard.

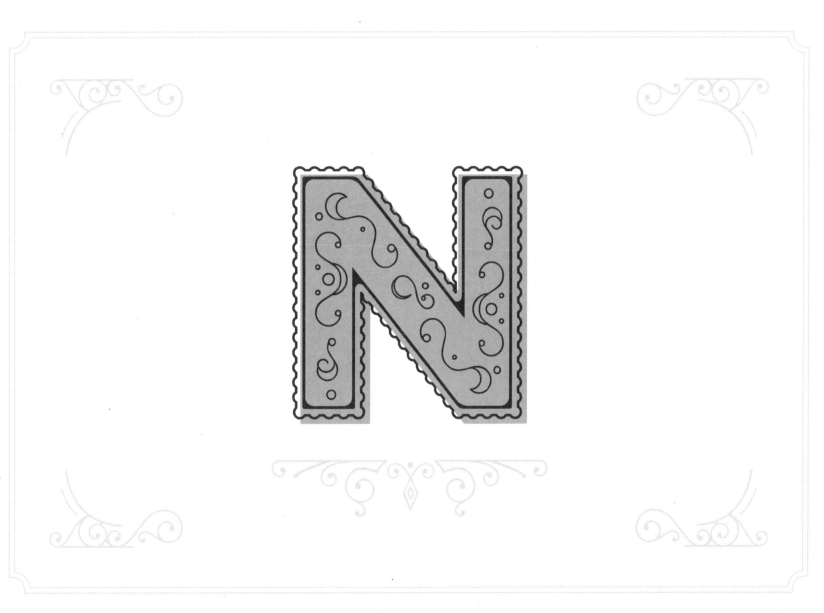

naked

adj. *without covering*

in the altogether

nekkid

without a stitch

as a jaybird

SUNNY JUNE WAS NEKKID AS A JAYBIRD.

NOW, USE IT IN A SENTENCE:

Uncle Jury went swimming in the altogether.

Mother Mamie was out in the yard without a stitch.

94

nervous

adj. *anxious*

as a long-tailed
cat in a roomful
of rocking chairs

fit to be tied

jumpy as spit on
a hot skillet

keyed up

on pins and needles

she's chewing her bit

skittish

NOW, USE IT IN A SENTENCE:

REBA JO WAS NERVOUS AS A LONG-TAILED CAT IN A ROOMFUL OF ROCKING CHAIRS!

Fred was jumpy as spit on a hot skillet when he lost his glasses.

Shaylene was keyed up before her presentation.

Frankie was on pins and needles about the test.

NERVOUS AS SPIT ON A HOT SKILLET

MEANING:

Very nervous, also used with "jumpy as."

FOR EXAMPLE:

"Virginia's play opens tonight. She is nervous as spit on a hot skillet."

ORIGIN:

This phrase is used in a variety of ways—some people says "jumpy as spit on a hot skillet," while others say "nervous as grease on a hot skillet."

Although we didn't find dates, the origins of this phrase are easy to deduce: Grease and tepid liquid (like saliva) sizzle and pop when they hit a hot skillet, seeming to jump.

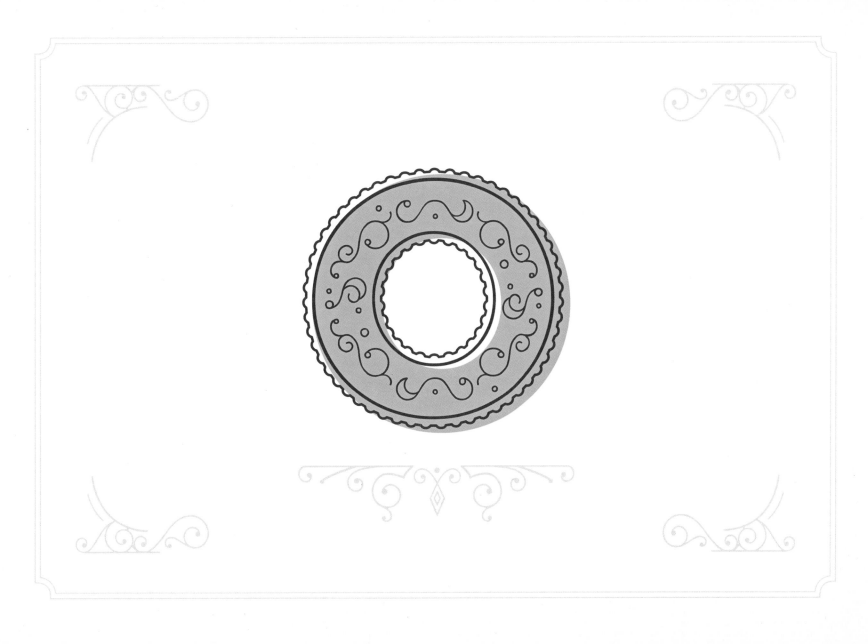

odiferous

adj. *stinky*

bad enough to
gag a maggot

bad enough to
knock a buzzard
off a gut wagon

stinks to
high heaven

THE LOCKER ROOM SMELLED BAD ENOUGH TO GAG A MAGGOT.

NOW, USE IT IN A SENTENCE:

The odor in Johnny Paul's room would knock a buzzard off a gut wagon.　　　*Shirlene's feet stink to high heaven.*

over there

prep. phrase, *beyond*

a fur piece

a good ways off

in the boonies

in the sticks

yonder

yonder ways

THEY LIVE WAY OUT IN THE BOONIES.

NOW, USE IT IN A SENTENCE:

The cabin was a good ways off the road.   *He lived out in the sticks.*   *The spooky old house was over yonder ways.*

overturn

v. *flip over*

tump

tump out

upend

upset

NOW, USE IT IN A SENTENCE:

Don't upset the wheelbarrow.

Did you upend the cart?

BE CAREFUL OR YOU'LL TUMP OUT THE GROCERIES.

overweight

adj. *heavier than average*

if he were an inch
taller, he'd be round

spread out like a
church supper

spread out
like a picnic

stout as a mule

weighs heavy

NOW, USE IT IN A SENTENCE:

If he were an inch taller, he'd be round.

Earline is spread out like a church supper.

JIMMY HAS GOTTEN TO BE STOUT AS A MULE EVER SINCE SANDY RAY STARTED COOKING FOR HIM.

WORDS THAT MEAN SOMETHING COMPLETELY DIFFERENT IN THE SOUTH

Everyone in the South knows we shop at the grocery store with a "buggy," rather than a "shopping cart." And when we say someone is "ugly," we're more often than not referring to a person's behavior rather than appearance. Here are some words that mean something completely different down here:

Barbecue

WHAT IT MEANS EVERYWHERE ELSE:
Grilling in the backyard.

WHAT IT MEANS IN THE SOUTH:
1. A type of slow-cooked meat typically served with baked beans on the side.

2. A favorite sauce that leads to more family arguments than politics.

Cut

WHAT IT MEANS EVERYWHERE ELSE:
Make an opening, incision or wound with a sharp-edged tool or object; to remove something using a sharp object.

WHAT IT MEANS IN THE SOUTH:
To turn off something.

Example: "Cut off the lights."

Mash

WHAT IT MEANS EVERYWHERE ELSE:
To crush, grind or squish.

Example: To make mashed potatoes.

WHAT IT MEANS IN THE SOUTH:
To press a button.

Example: "Ernest mashed the elevator button."

Buggy

WHAT IT MEANS EVERYWHERE ELSE:
An antiquated mode of transportation pulled by horses.

WHAT IT MEANS IN THE SOUTH:
1. A cart at the grocery store or Walmart.
2. What your windshield gets as you drive south toward the beach.

Coke

WHAT IT MEANS EVERYWHERE ELSE:
An abbreviation of Coca-Cola.

WHAT IT MEANS IN THE SOUTH:
Any carbonated beverage, including Coca-Cola.

Directly

WHAT IT MEANS EVERYWHERE ELSE:
To go straight to.

WHAT IT MEANS IN THE SOUTH:
Pretty soon.
Example: "I'll be there directly."

Reckon

WHAT IT MEANS EVERYWHERE ELSE:
To "settle accounts."

WHAT IT MEANS IN THE SOUTH:
"I suppose," "I think" or "I guess."

Spell

WHAT IT MEANS EVERYWHERE ELSE:
To put letters together to form a word.

WHAT IT MEANS IN THE SOUTH:
1. To feel faint or lightheaded.
Example: "Aunt Verna had one of her spells when Uncle Sid came home drunk."

2. Measure of time.
Example: "Come up on the porch and sit a spell."

Sugar

WHAT IT MEANS EVERYWHERE ELSE:
A sweetener.

WHAT IT MEANS IN THE SOUTH:
A kiss.

Toboggan

WHAT IT MEANS EVERYWHERE ELSE:
A snow sled.

WHAT IT MEANS IN THE SOUTH:
A skull cap, often worn while riding a snow sled.

Ugly

WHAT IT MEANS EVERYWHERE ELSE:
An unattractive person.

WHAT IT MEANS IN THE SOUTH:
To behave in a manner that is unbecoming.

Carry

WHAT IT MEANS EVERYWHERE ELSE:
To take objects in your arms and move them elsewhere.

WHAT IT MEANS IN THE SOUTH:
To transport to another place via motorized vehicle.
Example: "We had to carry Mama to the hospital last night."

PLAYING POSSUM

MEANING:

To lie still as if playing dead.

FOR EXAMPLE:

"Fred's not asleep; he's just playing possum."

ORIGIN:

We all know that to play possum means to "play dead." It has been in use since the early 17th century. And most of us know that's because possums play dead when threatened by a predator.

But did you know why and how a possum plays dead?

Surprisingly, possums don't play dead like humans do. Their bodies are equipped to make their fake deaths look as real as possible, according to the Opossum Society. "The opossum has an involuntary comatose-like state induced by extreme fear," the Society's website says. "Predators find 'the kill' part of the stimulus to eat; therefore, an inert opossum does nothing to excite their appetite, and they will leave it alone. Somehow the opossum's body knows when the danger has passed, and the opossum 'comes to' again."

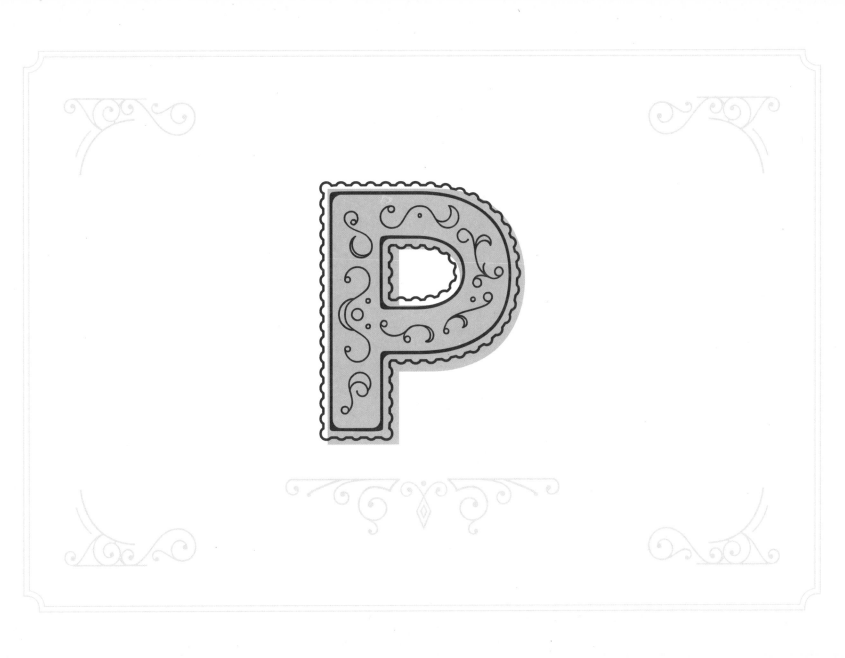

pants

n. *clothing to cover legs*

britches

coveralls

drawers

overalls

WEAR YOUR GOOD DRAWERS IN CASE YOU'RE IN AN ACCIDENT.

NOW, USE IT IN A SENTENCE:

His britches don't fit very well.

Grandpa always wears his coveralls in the garden.

pass out

v. *become unconscious*

fall out

have a spell

swoon

RENETTA WAS SO EXCITED SHE ABOUT FELL OUT.

NOW, USE IT IN A SENTENCE:

I'm so tired I'm about to fall out.

Mother nearly had a spell when she saw the price.

He was so handsome, Scarlett swooned.

PLUMB TUCKERED OUT

MEANING:

Extremely tired.

FOR EXAMPLE:

"I can't do yoga right now. I'm plumb tuckered out."

ORIGIN:

"Tuckered out," meaning "very tired," is not often used alone. The word "plumb" is used in front of it as "an intensifier," Phrases.org says. Other intensifiers used with the phrase are "clear," or "well-nigh."

It became popular in Western films of the 1930s and 1940s, making it popular for rural and country usage.

The word "tucker" is a colloquial New England word from the early 19th century, meaning "become weary."

poor, broke

adj. *lacking sufficient money*

as a church mouse

so poor I can't afford to pay attention

so poor I couldn't jump over a nickel to save a dime

too poor to paint, too proud to whitewash

without a pot to piss in or a window to throw it out of

JULIA WAS SO POOR SHE COULDN'T AFFORD TO PAY ATTENTION.

NOW, USE IT IN A SENTENCE:

The Joneses were too poor to paint, too proud to whitewash.

Sammy didn't have a pot to piss in or a window to throw it out of.

pretty

adj. *attractive*

comely

cute as a bug's ear

fetching

pretty as a peach

rather watch her walk
than eat fried chicken

more curves than
a barrel of snakes

THAT JANET IS PRETTY AS A PEACH.

NOW, USE IT IN A SENTENCE:

Dooley's girl was quite comely.   *Her new dress was fetching.*   *He would rather watch her walk than eat fried chicken.*

procrastinate

v. *delay, put off*

dawdle

dilly-dally

lollygag

mosey

HEATH WILL JUST MOSEY ALONG ON HIS OWN SWEET TIME.

NOW, USE IT IN A SENTENCE:

If you don't stop dawdling, we're going to be late.

Maude is known to lollygag.

Frank always dilly-dallied on the walk home.

punish

v. penalize for wrongdoing

cut a switch

jerk a knot in your tail

tan your hide

NOW, USE IT IN A SENTENCE:

Y'all stop arguing or I'll cut a switch.

IF YOU BREAK THAT, I'LL JERK A KNOT IN YOUR TAIL.

JERK A KNOT IN YOUR TAIL

MEANING:

A threat to punish someone.

FOR EXAMPLE:

"Kids, if you draw on that wall again, I'm going to jerk a knot in your tails."

ORIGIN:

This phrase is popular in the South and likely originated on horse farms because horses' tails get tangled in knots if they aren't brushed, according to TexasMonthly.com. No one wants to try jerking a horse's tail to get the knots out – he might just bite you.

purse

n. *tote for carrying personal items*

carryall

handbag

pocketbook

NOW, USE IT IN A SENTENCE:

It was hard to find anything in that huge carryall.

Janice had her husband hold her handbag while she tried on clothes.

BIG MAMA'S POCKETBOOK ALWAYS MATCHED HER SHOES WHEN SHE WENT TO CHURCH.

PREACHING TO THE CHOIR

MEANING:

A pointless endeavor.

FOR EXAMPLE:

"Yeah, the crops need some rain, but you're preaching to the choir."

ORIGIN:

Refers to the fact that members of the church choir are already among the faithful and don't require converting. In other words, you're telling someone who already knows. The first known reference is found in the *Lima News* in Ohio in 1973, says Grammarist.com.

THE SOUTHERN DEFINITION OF A "MESS"

"Mess" was already a seriously multitasking word before we Southerners decided to add to its workload.

It could mean "disordered, untidy or unpleasant condition," i.e., "the room is a mess."

It could mean "a place where people gather to eat," as in "lunch is in the mess hall."

It can even mean "a large quantity or number," as in "cooking a mess of collard greens."

Then we had to go complicate things by describing people as "a mess" – in a good way ... *and* in a bad way. So how do you tell the difference?

Here's the nice way to say it:

"Edna's oldest boy is such a mess!"

And the *mean* way:

"Edna's oldest boy is such a mess!"

See the difference? No?

That's because the difference in use of this word is all about nuances. Listen to tone, watch facial expressions. In the first example, the person talking about Edna's boy would be shaking her head and smiling, as if she finds it hard to believe just how cute and funny and *smart* that boy is.

In the second example, the person talking about Edna's boy would be shaking her head in sympathy, maybe adding a "tsk" and a "bless his heart" at the end because that boy apparently can't get his life together and he's disgracing the family.

Got it? See? That wasn't so difficult. Just practice your tone before you try this in public. Remember, God don't like ugly.

quickly

adj. *fast*

faster than
double-struck lightning

going flat-out

going wide open

lickety-split

like a scalded cat

like a scalded haint

like a shot

HE FLEW AT HER
LIKE A
SCALDED HAINT.

NOW, USE IT IN A SENTENCE:

He lit out of there faster than double-struck lightning.

That cat was off like a shot when it started to rain.

That car was going flat-out when it hit the highway.

rainstorm

n. *downpour of water, precipitation*

blowin' up a storm

frog-strangler

gully-washer

raining cats and dogs

NOW, USE IT IN A SENTENCE:

Grab your umbrella. It's blowin' up a storm.

It was coming down hard, a real frog-strangler.

Looks like we're in for a gully-washer.

IT'S RAINING CATS AND DOGS OUT HERE!

relatives

n. *members of the family*

folks

kin

kinfolks

mama 'n'em

NOW, USE IT IN A SENTENCE:

I'd love to come meet your folks.

Who's your kin?

HOW ARE YOUR MAMA 'N'EM DOING?

roam

v. wander about

gallivant

gad about

hit the road

NOW, USE IT IN A SENTENCE:

Don't just gad about. Get to work.

Daddy 'n'em hit the road to Florida.

JUNIOR WAS OUT GALLIVANTING AGAIN.

ruined

adj. *destroyed*

gone to pot

rurnt

spoiled

NOW, USE IT IN A SENTENCE:

Those children are pure-dee rurnt.

Aunt Didi spoils them beyond their worth.

GRANDPA'S RECLINER HAS GONE TO POT.

RARIN' TO GO

MEANING:

Eager to start something or go somewhere.

FOR EXAMPLE:

"Bobby was just rarin' to go to the birthday party."

ORIGIN:

This colloquialism likely has its origins in the South, according to TexasMonthly.com. "Raring" may come from "rearing," which is defined as "to stand on one's hind legs." Because wild and undisciplined horses are known to rear when they are eager to go someplace, it may have evolved to "raring," which is almost always used without the G on the end.

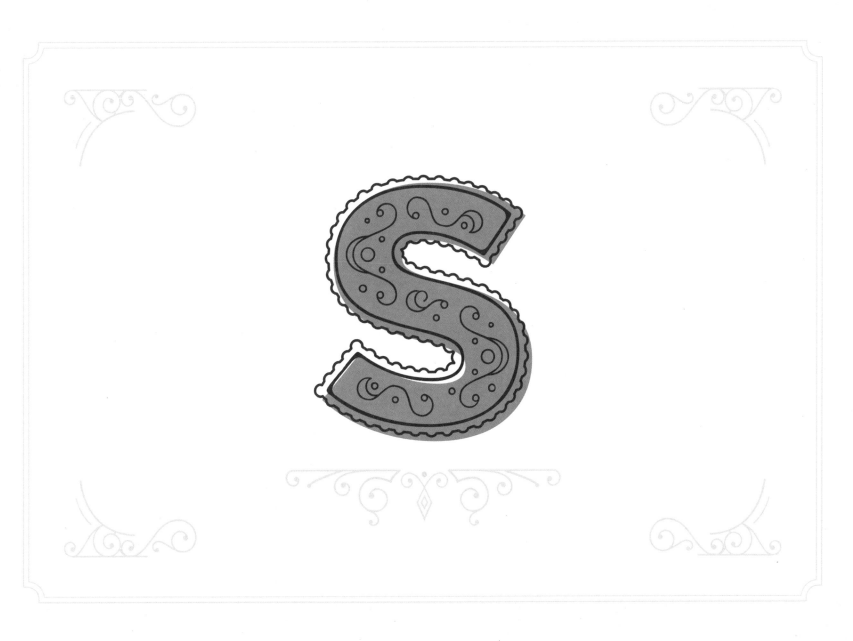

sad

adj. *unhappy, depressed*

in the doldrums

lower than a
gopher hole

out of sorts

sad enough to bring
a tear to a glass eye

so low I couldn't
jump off a dime

looks like the cheese
fell off his cracker

NOW, USE IT IN A SENTENCE:

BUBBA LOOKS LIKE THE CHEESE FELL OFF HIS CRACKER.

Sissy is lookin' lower than a gopher hole.   *I think Mama's out of sorts today.*   *Why, that movie would bring a tear to a glass eye.*

sauce

n. *condiment*

chocolate gravy

gravy

red-eye gravy

tomato gravy

white sauce

comeback sauce

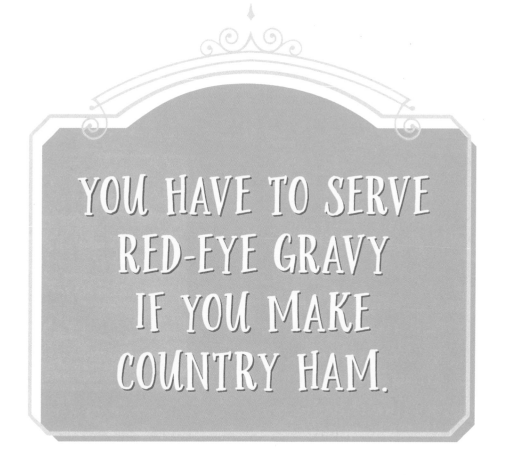

YOU HAVE TO SERVE RED-EYE GRAVY IF YOU MAKE COUNTRY HAM.

NOW, USE IT IN A SENTENCE:

Chocolate gravy is yummy on biscuits.

Barbecue pork and white sauce are a classic Southern combination.

scarce

adj. *insufficient, infrequent*

come up wanting

few and far between

scant

as hen's teeth

slim pickin's

FOUR-LEAF CLOVERS ARE FEW AND FAR BETWEEN.

NOW, USE IT IN A SENTENCE:

You keep spending so much and you'll come up wanting.

Your choice of sauces is scant.

Snowstorms are scarce as hen's teeth down here.

SCARCE AS HEN'S TEETH

MEANING:

Very scarce.

FOR EXAMPLE:

"His manners are scarce as hen's teeth."

ORIGIN:

First recorded during the Civil War, this phrase comes from the fact that, obviously, hens don't have teeth, according to the Free Dictionary.

scared

adj. *frightened*

**as a cat at
the dog pound**

**as a sinner in
a cyclone**

**yellow as mustard,
but without the bite**

yellow-bellied

THAT STORM HAD ME AS SCARED AS A CAT AT THE DOG POUND.

NOW, USE IT IN A SENTENCE:

Frankie Joe is yellow as mustard, but without the bite.

He was too yellow-bellied to go into the haunted house.

130

sleazy

adj. *dishonest, disreputable*

can't trust him any farther than one can throw him

lower than a snake's belly

slicker than a slop jar

so low you have to look up to see hell

sorry

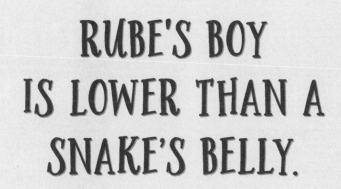

RUBE'S BOY IS LOWER THAN A SNAKE'S BELLY.

NOW, USE IT IN A SENTENCE:

You can't trust him any farther than you can throw him.

She's just sorry.

131

slow

adj. *unhurried, lazy*

a month of Sundays

dilly-dally

slower than a
Sunday afternoon

slower than
molasses in winter

VIVIAN MOVES SLOWER THAN MOLASSES IN WINTER.

NOW, USE IT IN A SENTENCE:

It would take a month of Sundays to paint the whole house.

With his walker, PopPop is slower than a Sunday afternoon.

small

adj. *tiny in size or quantity*

tee-tiny

little bitty

piddlin'

THERE WAS JUST A PIDDLIN' AMOUNT OF BANANA PUDDING LEFT.

NOW, USE IT IN A SENTENCE:

She was so tee-tiny you could hang her from a rearview mirror.

The backseat of his car was little bitty.

spunk

n. courage, nerve

gumption

moxie

pluck

IT TOOK SOME PLUCK FOR HER TO TRY GRITS IN CALIFORNIA.

NOW, USE IT IN A SENTENCE:

June Marie showed gumption when she stood up to Fred.

They always said Darlene was full of moxie.

stupid

adj. *not intelligent, irresponsible*

doesn't have sense
God gave a goose

half-witted

if brains were leather,
he couldn't saddle a flea

lunkheaded

thick as a
meatloaf sandwich

sharp as a mashed potato

NOW, USE IT IN A SENTENCE:

Harmon is about as thick as a meatloaf sandwich.

My brother is about as sharp as a mashed potato.

EMMA JEAN DOESN'T HAVE SENSE GOD GAVE A GOOSE.

suppose

v. to consider

dare say

hazard a guess

reckon

NOW, USE IT IN A SENTENCE:

I dare say Grandma's cornbread is the best.

If I had to hazard a guess, I'd say yes.

WILL IT RAIN TOMORROW, YOU RECKON?

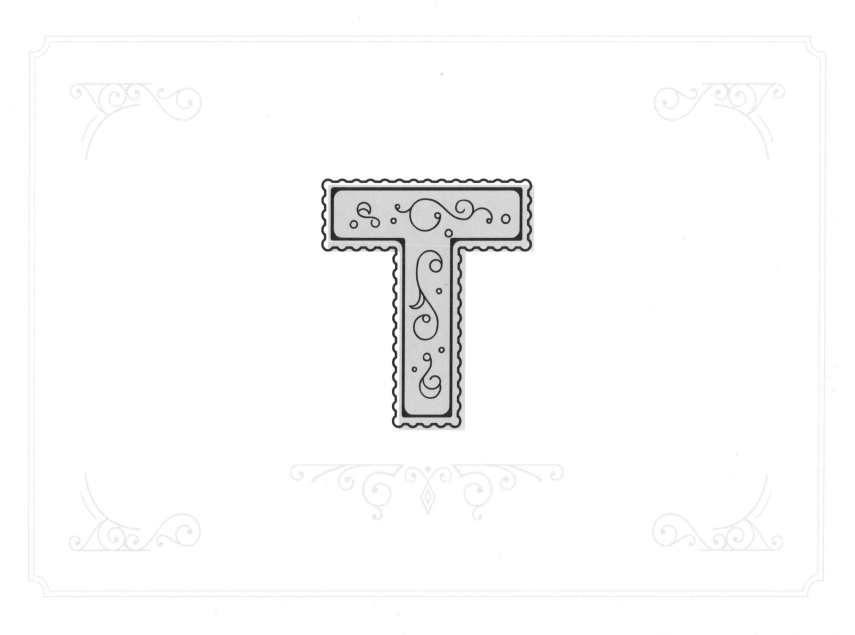

THAT DOG WON'T HUNT

MEANING:

An idea or plan that won't work.

FOR EXAMPLE:

"You really think you can jump that hay bale on your tractor? I say that dog won't hunt."

ORIGIN:

Came about in the 1800s because dogs are commonly used to hunt in the South, according to FreeDictionary.com. If the dog won't hunt, you are out of luck.

talkative

adj. *excessively communicative*

could talk a raccoon
right out of a tree

got a ten-gallon mouth

got tongue enough for
ten rows of teeth

long-winded

windy

THAT GIRL COULD TALK A RACCOON RIGHT OUT OF A TREE.

NOW, USE IT IN A SENTENCE:

The preacher sure was long-winded today.

That salesman's got tongue enough for ten rows of teeth.

tantrum

adj. *sudden burst of ill temper*

carry on

conniption

get your dander up

hissy fit

DALLY GOT HIS DANDER UP AND WENT AFTER TROY.

NOW, USE IT IN A SENTENCE:

She was just carryin' on right in the middle of the Walmarts.   *Granny had a conniption when Diddy mowed her azalea bush.*

CONNIPTION/HISSY FIT (TO HAVE/PITCH A)

MEANING:

To have a tantrum; get hysterical. A fit of temper, an angry outburst.

FOR EXAMPLE:

"Mother Maybell had a conniption fit when I used instant banana pudding."

"I'm getting your dinner. Don't pitch a hissy fit."

ORIGIN:

Conniption: May be related to "corruption," which was used to mean "anger" in the late 1700s, or "canapshus," meaning "ill-tempered," or "captious," meaning an ill-natured person, according to WordWizard.com.

Hissy fit: The word "hissy" is related to the word "hysterics," according to WritingExplained.org. It may also refer to the hiss or stutter someone makes when angry. In use since the 1930s.

temperamental

adj. *angry, moody*

crotchety

nitpicky

persnickety

touchy

THERE'S NO NEED TO BE SO TOUCHY ABOUT IT.

NOW, USE IT IN A SENTENCE:

Our neighbor is just a crotchety old man.

Pearline was just too persnickety for words.

The teacher was nitpicky about the assignment.

throw

v. propel something through the air

chuck

chunk

let fly

NOW, USE IT IN A SENTENCE:

Just chuck that in the trash.

He just let fly the ax and cut the tree clean in two.

YOU CAN CHUNK THOSE LEFTOVERS OUT.

toilet

v. *bathroom*

commode

outhouse

privy

THEY STILL HAD A LITTLE WOODEN PRIVY BEHIND THE HOUSE.

NOW, USE IT IN A SENTENCE:

You'll have to clean the commode again. Uncle Hugh was just in there.   *The old outhouse is one of the historic structures on the farm.*

toys

n. *an object for children to play with*

play-pretties

playthings

trifles

NOW, USE IT IN A SENTENCE:

Company's coming. Y'all pick up your play-pretties from the living room floor.

Put your trifles back in the toy box.

YOU KIDS HAVE STREWN YOUR PLAYTHINGS ALL OVER THE HOUSE.

WHAT THE WORD

– TACKY –

MEANS IN THE SOUTH

Use of the word "tacky" to mean gaudy began in the South, although its usage has since crept into other regions. Author Pat Conroy said in *The Lords of Discipline:* "It's impossible to explain to a Yankee what 'tacky' is. They simply have no word for it up north, but my God, do they ever need one."

So how did a word that refers to stickiness come to mean something that is gaudy or garish or lacking in taste?

It likely originated with a breed of horse. According to Dictionary.com, many linguists believe the wild Carolina Marsh Tacky horses are responsible for the word because they were considered to have "a lack of breeding." The word became a description well-to-do Southerners used to describe anyone they considered "trashy." From there, the word evolved to mean "in poor taste."

Here are just a few things that might be considered "tacky":

* Bad manners;

* Not pulling over for a funeral procession;

* Talking back to Meemaw;

* Using curse words on social media.

Today, Marsh Tacky horses are rare, but the word "tacky" is going strong. Remember the main rule when using the word "tacky": You can think someone's outfit is tacky – you can even say it aloud to the person next to you, if you add the obligatory "bless her heart." But you shouldn't go around later telling the entire town her outfit was tacky and you should never, ever say it directly to the person whose outfit was tacky. Because that would be tacky.

ugly

adj. *unattractive*

as homemade sin

eat up with ugly

fell out of the ugly tree
and hit every branch
on the way down

looks like 10 miles
of bad road

not much to look at

make a freight train
take a dirt road

so ugly could throw a
buzzard off a gut pile

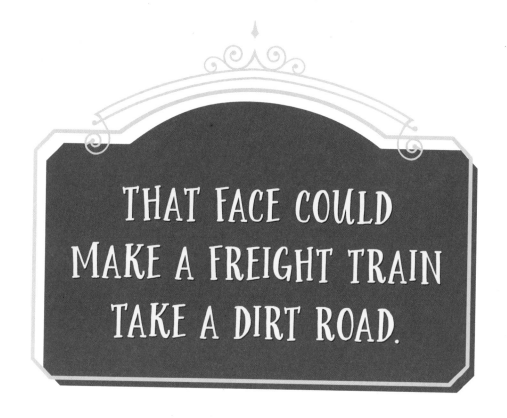

THAT FACE COULD
MAKE A FREIGHT TRAIN
TAKE A DIRT ROAD.

NOW, USE IT IN A SENTENCE:

Janna's boy was just eat up with ugly, bless his heart.

After working a double shift, Lulu looked like 10 miles of bad road.

underwear

*n. clothing worn under
outer clothes*

long handles

long johns

step-ins

underbritches

underpants

unmentionables

GET OUT YOUR LONG HANDLES FOR THE WINTER.

NOW, USE IT IN A SENTENCE:

Mama says put on clean underbritches before going out.

She didn't like to buy (whisper) unmentionables at the dollar store.

upset

adj. *bothered*

get one's feathers ruffled

tore up

to have a come-apart

HE WAS JUST TORE UP AFTER THE DIVORCE.

NOW, USE IT IN A SENTENCE:

Nana tends to get her feathers ruffled when people come by unannounced.

The news made Francine have a come-apart.

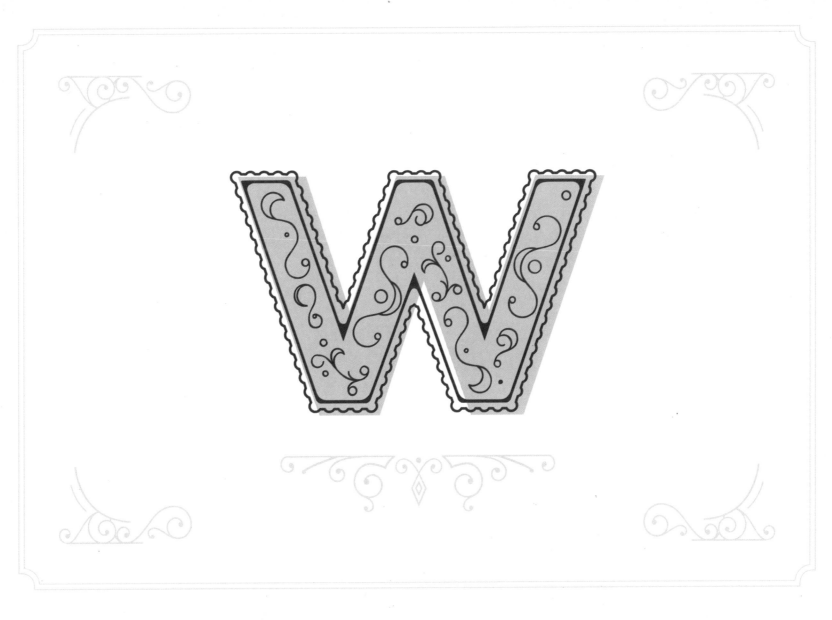

wow

exclamation

butter my butt and
call me a biscuit

I swan

if that don't beat all

slap my head and
call me silly

NOW, USE IT IN A SENTENCE:

As Grandma used to say, "Well, I swan!"

*It snowed 2 inches last night;
if that don't beat all!*

WELL, BUTTER MY BUTT
AND CALL ME A BISCUIT!

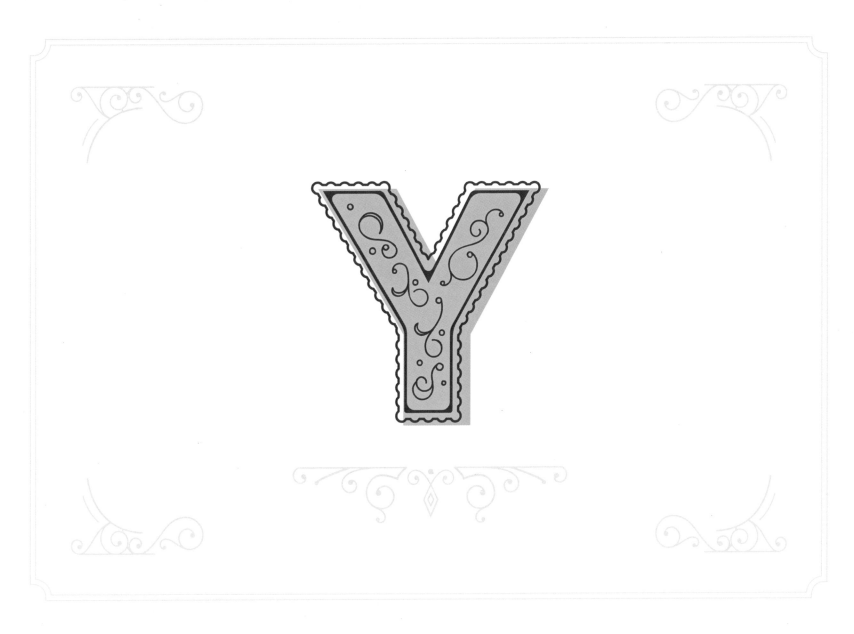

you

*pronoun of the second
person singular or plural*

y'all

all y'all

NOW, USE IT IN A SENTENCE:

*Hey, Sue, can I ride with
y'all to the store?*

ARE ALL Y'ALL GOING TO THE FAMILY REUNION?

YOU CAN HANG YOUR HAT ON IT

MEANING:

To believe or depend on something.

FOR EXAMPLE:

"That's a promise you can hang your hat on."

ORIGIN:

This phrase is used a lot in Texas, which is likely because so many Texans wear hats. The date of its origin is unclear, TexasMonthly.com says. It comes from the fact that a person would only hang a heavy cowboy hat on a sturdy rack. In other words, if the place where you hang your hat is unreliable, your hat will fall to the floor.

Be sure to visit the
It's a Southern Thing store!

We celebrate Southern culture with fun shirts and gifts, children's picture books and family games, such as *Just Like Mama Used to Say* and *That Dog Won't Hunt*.

Store.SouthernThing.com

About the Author

Kelly Kazek, an award-winning journalist and humor columnist, writes about the South's culture for *It's a Southern Thing* and *This is Alabama*. She is the author of two humor books, five children's picture books and numerous books of regional history. She lives near Huntsville, Alabama, with her Sasquatch-sized husband, Sweetums.

About the Illustrator

Joshua J. Hamilton is an illustrator and Emmy-nominated filmmaker. He currently works as senior video producer for *It's a Southern Thing*. In 2020, Joshua was awarded a fellowship grant from the Alabama State Council on the Arts in media/photography for his documentary film work. He currently lives in Tuscaloosa, Alabama, with his wife, Emily.

It's a Southern Thing serves up relatable humor, inspirational people and fascinating stories that break the stereotypes and show the South as the culturally rich, diverse, down-home place it really is. Visit us at *southernthing.com* and find us on Facebook, YouTube, Instagram, TikTok and Twitter.